NORSE MYTHOLOGY

DRAGONS
OF NORSE MYTHOLOGY

BY AMY C. REA

Kids Core

An Imprint of Abdo Publishing
abdobooks.com

abdobooks.com

Published by Abdo Publishing, a division of ABDO, PO Box 398166, Minneapolis, Minnesota 55439. Copyright © 2024 by Abdo Consulting Group, Inc. International copyrights reserved in all countries. No part of this book may be reproduced in any form without written permission from the publisher. Kids Core™ is a trademark and logo of Abdo Publishing.

Printed in the United States of America, North Mankato, Minnesota.
052023
092023

Cover Photo: Shutterstock Images
Interior Photos: Shutterstock Images, 4–5, 18; Chronicle/Alamy, 7, 9, 28 (top); Historic Images/Alamy, 10; AF Fotografie/Alamy, 12–13, 17, 29 (bottom); INTERFOTO/Alamy, 15, 29 (top); Barry Chin/The Boston Globe/Getty Images, 20–21; DeAgostini/De Agostini Editorial/Getty Images, 23; Werner Forman/Universal Images Group/Getty Images, 25; John Morrison/Alamy, 26; The History Collection/Alamy, 28 (bottom)

Editor: Katharine Hale
Series Designer: Katharine Hale

Library of Congress Control Number: 2022949111

Publisher's Cataloging-in-Publication Data

Names: Rea, Amy C., author.
Title: Dragons of Norse mythology / by Amy C. Rea
Description: Minneapolis, Minnesota: Abdo Publishing Company, 2024 | Series: Norse mythology | Includes online resources and index.
Identifiers: ISBN 9781098291167 (lib. bdg.) | ISBN 9781098277345 (ebook)
Subjects: LCSH: Mythology, Norse--Juvenile literature. | Dragons--Juvenile literature. | Animals, Mythical--Juvenile literature. | Fictitious animals--Juvenile literature.
Classification: DDC 293.13--dc23

CONTENTS

Jormungandr is a dragon from Norse mythology.

CHAPTER 1

NORSE DRAGONS

Jormungandr (YOHR-muhn-gan-der) was a long, snakelike dragon. The god Odin heard a **prophecy** that Jormungandr and his siblings were dangerous. So Odin wanted to destroy them. Odin threw Jormungandr into the sea.

Jormungandr was scared as he fell and splashed into the sea. But he did not die when he hit the water. Instead, he grew until he was enormous. He could wrap his body around Earth, known as Midgard, and put his tail in his mouth. People called Jormungandr the Midgard **Serpent**. He waited for Ragnarok, or the end of the world. Then he would rise up with his siblings to fight the gods.

Jormungandr's Family

Jormungandr had an interesting family. His father was Loki, the **trickster** god. His mother was a giantess named Angrboda. He had a brother and a sister. Fenrir was a large wolf. Hel was the queen of the dead. Odin and the gods were scared of all three siblings.

Stories say Jormungandr and Thor will fight and kill each other at Ragnarok.

Norse Mythology

The religion of early northern Germanic peoples is known today as Norse mythology. Most surviving Norse myths come from **Scandinavia**. They are written in the Old Norse language.

The Norse people believed that life on Earth had cycles. That meant Earth was created and would be destroyed. The world would end in the flames of Ragnarok. But Ragnarok would lead to the birth of a new planet. The cycle would start all over again.

Holder of the Nine Worlds

Norse mythology says the universe is made of nine worlds. These worlds are held together by Yggdrasil (IHG-druh-sihl). Yggdrasil is an enormous tree. The tree is so big that its top goes above the clouds. Yggdrasil needs to be kept healthy for the nine worlds to survive.

In Norse mythology, a rainbow bridge called the Bifrost connects Midgard to the land of the gods.

In one Norse myth, the god Thor and a giant named Hymir go fishing together, and Thor catches Jormungandr.

In Norse mythology, the nine worlds are home to many types of creatures. Besides the gods, there are humans, giants, dwarfs, and elves. There are also dragons. In some stories, the dragons were born as dragons. Other dragons changed later in life. The dragons were very powerful. The Norse people believed dragons brought evil and chaos into the world. They thought dragons could destroy Yggdrasil and the nine worlds.

Explore Online

Visit the website below. Does it give any new information about Odin that wasn't in Chapter One?

Odin

abdocorelibrary.com/dragons-of-norse-mythology

The story of Sigurd slaying the dragon Fafnir is a famous Norse myth.

CHAPTER 2

THE POWER OF DRAGONS

Dragons were often called serpents in Norse myths. The Old Norse language called them *ormr*, which translates to "serpent." Later, the language changed. The creatures were called *dreki*, which translates to "dragon."

Jormungandr was not the only dragon in Norse mythology. There were two other important dragons. All three had key roles in the stories.

Nidhogg

Nidhogg was a fierce dragon who lived under Yggdrasil. He was known as the dragon of the dead. He stayed beneath Yggdrasil and fed on dead murderers, liars, and cheaters. He also nibbled on Yggdrasil's roots. The Norse people believed this would make the tree turn yellow and start to die. Then Ragnarok would begin. Nidhogg would rise from the roots and lead an army of giants to fight the gods.

Nidhogg's Home

Eagle
A wise eagle
The hawk Vedrfolnir sits between the eagle's eyes.

Ratatoskr
A messenger squirrel
Sometimes he spreads gossip and lies, making Nidhogg and the eagle angry with each other.

Nidhogg
A dragon
He chews on Yggdrasil's roots.

Norse mythology says an eagle lives in Yggdrasil's highest branches. A squirrel called Ratatoskr runs up and down Yggdrasil's trunk, passing messages between Nidhogg and the eagle.

Fafnir

Heidmar was the king of the dwarfs. He had three sons. They were Fafnir, Otr, and Regin. Fafnir and Otr could change their bodies into animals. Regin was a **smith**.

Loki was the Norse **trickster** god. One day, Loki killed Otr while the dwarf was in the form of an otter. Heidmar and his sons demanded treasure to make up for Otr's death. Loki took the treasure from another dwarf. His name was Andvari. One of the treasures was a golden ring. Andvari was angry about losing his treasure. He cursed the ring to bring misery and death to its owner.

Fafnir killed his father to get the treasure. Then he turned himself into a poison-breathing

In some versions of the story, Regin and Fafnir both kill their father. But Fafnir betrays Regin and does not share the gold.

dragon to protect it. Regin wanted the treasure too. He told his **foster son** Sigurd to kill Fafnir so Regin could have the treasure. Sigurd killed the dragon for Regin.

Sigurd went on to have many other adventures in Norse mythology.

But Regin was also greedy. He planned to kill Sigurd for the treasure. Sigurd learned of the plan and killed Regin first. Fafnir's myth shows that greed leads to anger and death.

J. R. R. Tolkien

The Norse myths continue to inspire writers. One of these writers was J. R. R. Tolkien. A fierce dragon called Smaug appears in his novel *The Hobbit*. Smaug is based on Fafnir. The ring from *The Hobbit* and *Lord of the Rings* is inspired by the cursed ring in Fafnir's story.

Fafnismal, or the Tale of Fafnir, is an Old Norse poem. After Sigurd kills Fafnir, the dragon gives the man a warning about his cursed treasure.

> *Take my advice,*
>
> *and ride home from here.*
>
> *My clanging gold . . .*
>
> *will bring about your death.*

Source: Jackson Crawford, translator. *The Poetic Edda: Stories of the Norse Gods and Heroes,* Hackett, 2015, p. 245.

What's the Big Idea?

Read this quote carefully. What is its main idea? Explain how the main idea is supported by details.

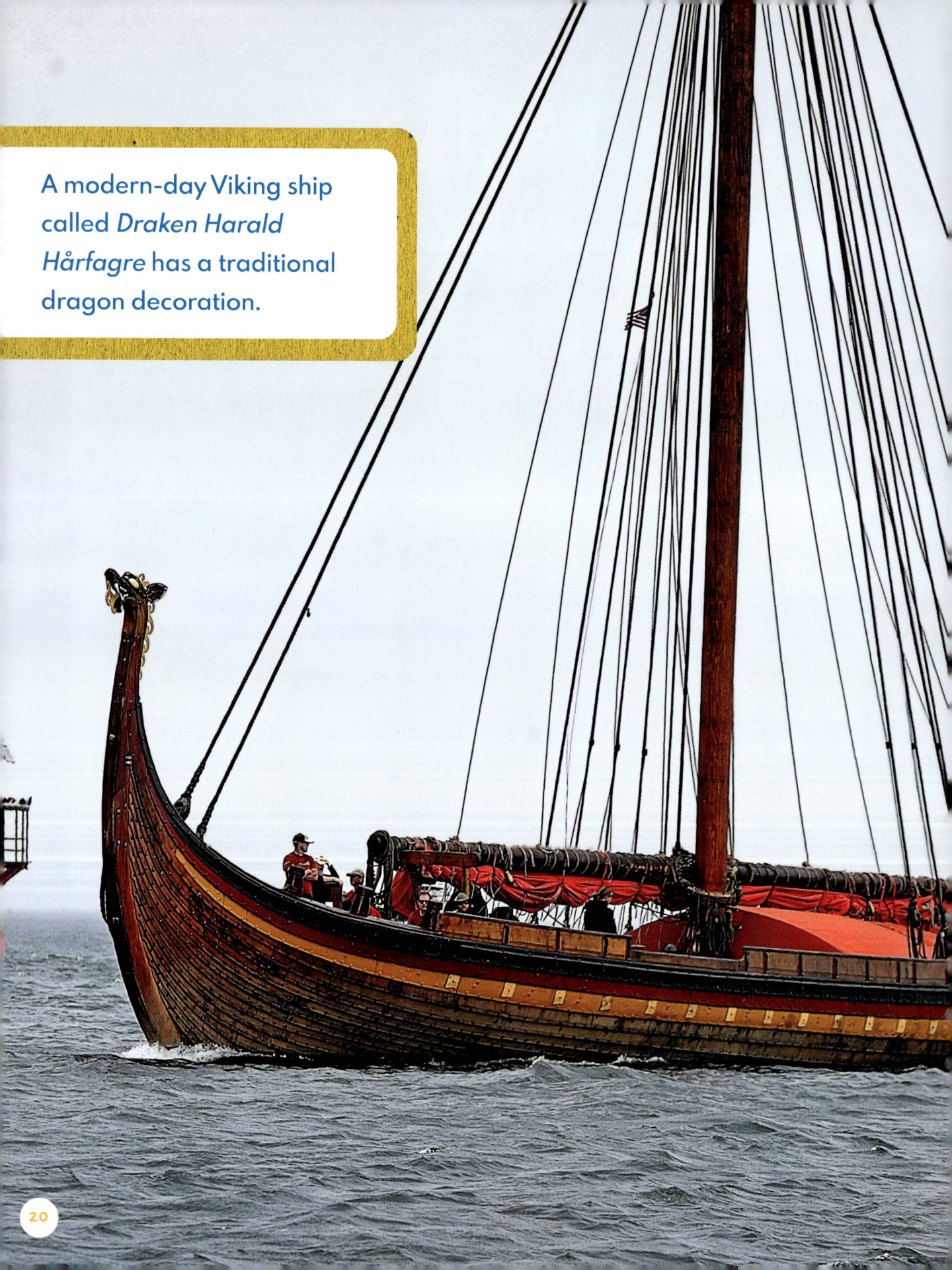

A modern-day Viking ship called *Draken Harald Hårfagre* has a traditional dragon decoration.

CHAPTER 3

THE MEANING OF DRAGONS

The Norse people created many pieces of art. They would decorate furniture and other objects with scenes from Norse mythology. In early Norse artwork, dragons looked different from how most European people imagine dragons today.

The dragons did not always breathe fire or have wings. Sometimes they had only two legs rather than four. They were long, thin creatures. That is why they were called serpents in the earliest myths.

Vikings were warriors and sailors who came from Scandinavia. They lived from the 800s to the mid-1000s CE. Vikings built ships to sail to other countries. They used the ships to raid other countries and bring back valuable things. When they built their ships, they sometimes carved a large wooden dragon's head into the front. This was meant to scare the people they wanted to raid. Vikings also believed the heads had magical powers. Those powers would protect the Vikings from evil spirits.

Vikings carved and placed rune stones to honor the dead. Some rune stones, such as this one found in Jelling, Denmark, show dragons.

Death and Chaos

In the Norse myths, dragons were **symbols** of death and chaos. But the Norse people did not see this as a bad thing. They believed the dragons were a necessary part of the cycle of life. Dragons would have a key role in Ragnarok.

The Stenkyrka Stone

Norse picture stones are large stone tablets with carved images. The stones help historians learn more about Norse people of the Viking age. Many stones have been found on the Swedish island of Gotland. The Stenkyrka Smiss stone is from the 800s or 900s CE. Its carvings show a Viking ship. The front of the ship is a dragon's head. The back is the dragon's tail.

Stave churches were large wooden churches common in northern Europe. In the 1100s, an artist carved Sigurd's story into the doorway of the Hylestad stave church in Norway.

The Gosforth Cross is a Viking cross found in a churchyard in England. Some scholars think the cross shows scenes from Ragnarok.

Ragnarok had to happen for a new world to begin. The dragons were part of the destruction cycle. They were necessary to complete the old cycle and start a new one. Dragons were important to the Norse people. They were fearful creatures. But they were a necessary part of life.

Further Evidence

Look at the website below. Does it give any new evidence to support Chapter Two?

How to Spot a Dragon: Five Dragons from Around the World

abdocorelibrary.com/dragons-of -norse-mythology

LEGENDARY FACTS

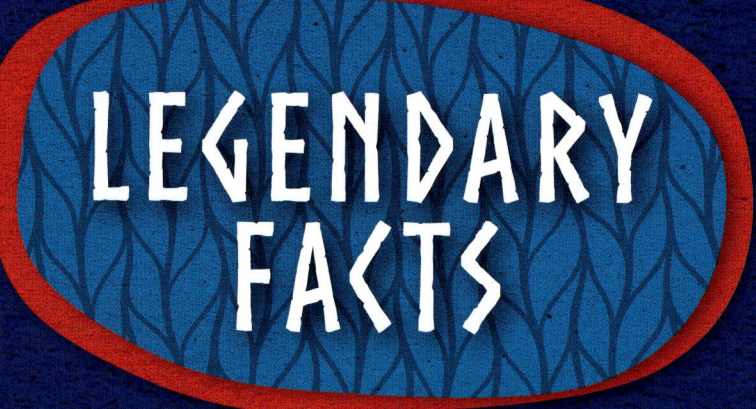

In Norse mythology, Ragnarok is the final battle at the end of the world. Dragons will play key roles in Ragnarok.

Jormungandr is called the Midgard Serpent. After Odin threw him into the sea, he grew until he could encircle Midgard, or Earth.

Nidhogg is a dragon who lives at the base of Yggdrasil, the tree of life. He nibbles on the tree's roots, which will lead to Ragnarok.

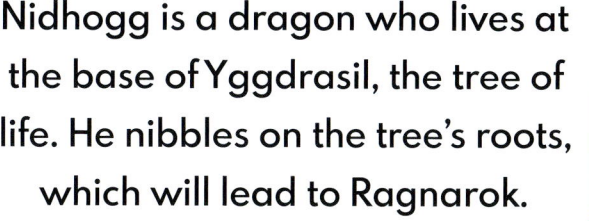

Fafnir was a dwarf who became a dragon to greedily guard his treasure. Fafnir's brother Regin encourages Sigurd to slay the beast so Regin can have the treasure.

Glossary

foster son
a boy who is temporarily cared for by someone who is not his birth parent

prophecy
a prediction of something that will happen in the future

Scandinavia
the countries of Norway, Sweden, and Denmark, and sometimes Iceland and Finland

serpent
a snake

smith
a person who works with metal

symbols
pictures or items that represent something else

trickster
a person who plays pranks or tricks on someone else

Online Resources

To learn more about dragons of Norse mythology, visit our free resource websites below.

Visit **abdocorelibrary.com** or scan this QR code for free Common Core resources for teachers and students, including vetted activities, multimedia, and booklinks, for deeper subject comprehension.

Visit **abdobooklinks.com** or scan this QR code for free additional online weblinks for further learning. These links are routinely monitored and updated to provide the most current information available.

Learn More

Bell, Samantha S. *Dragons of Chinese Mythology*. Abdo, 2023.

Conley, Kate. *Loki*. Abdo, 2024.

Ralphs, Matt. *Norse Myths*. DK Children, 2021.

Index

About the Author

Amy C. Rea is the author of several children's books. She also writes about travel and food in Minnesota. She lives in Saint Anthony, Minnesota, with her husband and silly dog.